ABUSE: Bruised but Not Broken!

ABUSE: Bruised but Not Broken!

by
Cheryl Prewitt-Salem

Tulsa, Oklahoma

Unless otherwise indicated all New Testament Scripture quotations are taken from *The Amplified Bible, New Testament*, © 1954, 1958 by the Lockman Foundation, La Habra, California.

Unless otherwise indicated, all Old Testament Scripture quotations are taken from *The Amplified Bible, Old Testament*, © 1962, 1964 by Zondervan Publishing House, Grand Rapids, Michigan.

Verses marked KJV are taken from the *King James Version* of the Bible.

ABUSE: Bruised but Not Broken!
ISBN 0-89274-587-8
Copyright © 1989 by Cheryl Prewitt-Salem
P. O. Box 701287
Tulsa, Oklahoma 74170

Published by **Praise Books**
P. O. Box 35035
Tulsa, Oklahoma 74153

Printed in the United States of America.
All rights reserved under International Copyright Law. Contents and/or cover may not be reproduced in whole or in part in any form without the express written consent of the Publisher.

Acknowledgment

Special thanks to Jeanne Alcott who has been invaluable in helping me put my experiences, thoughts and teachings into this book to help you be an overcomer!

ABUSE: Bruised but Not Broken!

by Cheryl Prewitt-Salem

Introduction

The first thing I want to say to you in this book is that YOU ARE NOT ALONE! No matter what type of abuse you have been through — verbal, mental, physical or sexual — there are others who have been through it too or who are going through it now. Abuse does not happen to just certain types of people in certain types of situations in life. It happens to many, many people. Abuse is not just a problem among non-Christians — it's a problem of the Church also. In fact, abuse can happen in religious families.

Why am I telling you this? The reason you need to know that you are not alone is so you won't feel guilty. You must not feel that this is a big problem that you caused. Many people are innocent victims, as you are. You must realize this fact before you can rid yourself of the emotional scar the abuse has left in your life.

You may be thinking, "Oh, but Cheryl, you don't know what I have done; I deserved the abuse I received." Before you can go any further in your healing from abuse, you must realize that this is a lie from the devil. It is *never right* for you or anyone else to be abused. Even if you did something or said something that you feel brought on the abuse, you still did not deserve to be abused.

You were a *victim*. Abuse is an action against you...a violation against you. You must recognize it for what it is — abuse is destruction. It tears down. And the only way it can be counteracted is through victorious living in Jesus...and that takes practice.

But you must practice the right kind of victorious living!

Unfortunately, too many people practice and rehearse *negative* thoughts. Those thoughts come out of their mouth, go into their ears, then filter down into their heart, and the whole cycle starts over. The Word of God says that whatever is in your heart is what is going to come out of your mouth. (Matt. 12:34,35.)

The Bible also says that faith comes from hearing the Word. (Rom. 10:17.) Well, if faith can come from hearing the *positive*, then the opposite of faith (fear, depression, disappointment and discouragement) can come from hearing the *negative*. In other words, instead of hearing God's Word, you can listen to Satan's word — the negative. You may not think you are listening to his words, but if you are thinking negative thoughts, feeling guilty and worthless, those *are* the devil's thoughts — not God's.

God never condemns anyone, nor does He cause His creation, made in His likeness (Gen. 1:26), to feel unworthy. He gave His only Son, Jesus Christ, so that we ALL can believe on Him and become sons and daughters and joint-heirs with Him. (Rom. 8:17.) YOU ARE SOMEBODY* — you are worthy. You are a child of God.

That's why I have written this book — to give you the right steps to practice to get completely free of abuse and totally healed of its scar.

I *could* fill this book with many wonderful stories of how people have come through abuse, conquered it and been healed of it. A story is a wonderful thing, but when your life is in danger, when your very spirit and your very soul and your very physical body are in jeopardy, a nice story is not what you need. You must learn how to *fight*. You

---

*I encourage you to get more teaching on this subject. There is so much God has to say on it. Be sure to read Chapter 5, "Overcoming Hurts," in my book, *You Are Somebody*. (See order form in the back of this book.)

ABUSE: Bruised but Not Broken!

have to learn how to stand firm and strong against the devil. You have to learn who your enemy is and that you fight in the spiritual realm, not the physical. *You don't fight with flesh words, you fight with spirit words.*

It's great when you know you can stand strong against the devil (and make him shiver in his boots) by speaking the Word of God, the truth, out loud. It's not enough to just read it to yourself. You must speak it out loud — for yourself and for the devil. You see, the devil *cannot* read our minds. He may act as though he can, but he cannot. He can only read our *actions* and hear our *words!* So we must speak the Word of God out of our mouths when we want to speak against the devil.

I challenge you to go through just one day listening to yourself — to everything that comes out of your mouth. If you are having problems being healed of abuse or anything else in your life, I believe you'll find that you are helping to prevent your healing by the confessions you are speaking. What do you say when you look in the mirror? What do you say when you are alone? What do you say when everything is going wrong?

We need to learn to listen to ourselves and quit saying bad things but instead say good things. We must *speak out* the Word of God. We must say good things *out loud*. Remember: Don't tell God about your Big Problem; tell your problem about your *Big God!*

As harsh as it may sound, I believe that if you *really* want to get healed, you'll get serious about this issue of speaking forth the Word of God. If you don't want to do that, you'll stay sick. That's the bottom line.

No matter what the symptoms in your life may be, until you are healed of the emotional scar that was caused by abuse, you cannot be healed permanently. There are many "symptoms" of abuse (but, of course, not all the people who have these symptoms have been abused). The ones I'm going to discuss just happen to be some of the more evident symptoms of abuse.

Abuse victims often have a tendency to suffer from eating disorders such as anorexia, bulimia or obesity. Subconsciously they are saying to those who have abused them: "You may have abused my body, you may have abused me sexually, you may have abused me verbally, but you cannot control what I eat; so I will either eat myself into oblivion or starve myself to death." Their eating disorder is simply a reaction, a subconscious attempt to control something in their lives, even if it is just their weight or eating habits.

If you have any of these eating disorders, or any other symptoms of abnormal behavior, you must recognize that they can be caused by spirits that have gotten into your life because of the scars of the abuse you have suffered. The devil wants to use these disorders to cause you to have a suicidal spirit.

You may not be killing yourself by putting a gun to your head, but you're committing suicide slowly by either overeating or starving yourself to death. These and many other symptoms of less destructive behavior all come from the emotional scars of abuse.

It takes PRACTICE of God's Word to be healed and to keep your healing. As I mentioned earlier, this book gives you those things to practice, along with scriptures to read out loud. I've kept it as short as possible for one very important reason — I want you to be able to pick it up and read it quickly, then pick it up again the next day and reread it. Then perhaps read it once a week. As you do so, you will begin to recognize that you are getting healed more and more.

Yes, your healing is *possible*. But once you receive it, you must continually be aware that Satan will try to steal it. With these ten steps, and the scriptures I give you with each one, you can stand against the devil and be free of any bondage he tries to place on you. Read these ten steps carefully with an open heart, then put this book some place where you will have easy access to it.

Ten Steps to Wholeness

STEP 1: SEARCH YOURSELF (Be honest with yourself)

The first step in freeing yourself from the scars in your life is to open up and look at your life with honest eyes, ready to see the truth so you can let Jesus help you deal with it little by little, step by step.

Scriptures to confess:

Jeremiah 17:10: **I, the Lord, search the mind, I try the heart, even to give to every man according to his ways, according to the fruit of his doings.**

John 3:21: **But he who practices truth — who does what is right — comes out into the light....**

ABUSE: Bruised but Not Broken!

All things must come out into the light, and be faced by you! I am not talking about facing people. I'm talking about facing memories — facing the truth and being set free by your honesty with yourself.

STEP 2: KNOW YOURSELF (Learn who you are)

Get to know yourself. You are made in the image of God. The best way to get in touch with who you are is to get in touch with Who God is! Spend time with Him, letting Him hold you, love you and heal you.

Scriptures to confess:

Genesis 1:26,27: **God said, Let Us [Father, Son, and Holy Spirit] make mankind in Our image, after Our likeness; and let them have complete authority over the fish of the sea, the birds of the air, the [tame] beasts, and over all of the earth, and over every thing that creeps upon the earth.**

So God created man in His own image, in the image *and* likeness of God He created him; male and female He created them.

Genesis 3:22: **And the Lord God said, Behold, the man is become as one of Us [the Father, Son, and Holy Spirit], to know [how to distinguish between] good and evil, and blessing and calamity; and now, lest he put forth his hand and take also of the tree of life, and eat and live for ever —**

Genesis 5:1,2: **This is the book — the written record — of the generations of the off-spring of Adam. When God created man He made him in the likeness of God.**

He created them male and female and blessed them, and named them [both] Adam at the time they were created.

STEP 3: FORGIVE YOURSELF
(Release yourself by forgiving yourself)

Jesus has forgiven you. God the

Father has forgiven you. You must release yourself by forgiving yourself.

Scriptures to confess:

John 3:16: **For God so greatly loved *and* dearly prized the world that He [even] gave up His only-begotten (unique) Son, so that whoever believes in (trusts, clings to, relies on) Him shall not perish — come to destruction, be lost — but have eternal (everlasting) life.**

Romans 3:23: **Since all have sinned and are falling short of the honor *and* glory which God bestows *and* receives.**

1 John 1:9: **If we [freely] admit that we have sinned *and* confess our sins, He is faithful and just (true to His own nature and promises) and will forgive our sins [dismiss our lawlessness] and continuously cleanse us from all unrighteousness — everything not in conformity to His will in purpose, thought and action.**

STEP 4: FREE YOURSELF
(Pronounce yourself not guilty)

The best way to completely free yourself is to *choose*. Just make the choice to forgive the person (or people) who scarred your life by word and/or actions. Forgiveness is an *act* — an *action!* And *act*-ion is something you first have to *choose* to do — whether you feel like it or not. Speak forgiveness out of your mouth. You must *act* as though you have forgiven. Then after you have practiced the *act*-ion, it becomes natural. This exercise takes longer for some people than others, but if you will be faithful with the action, forgiveness will eventually "stick" to you!

Scriptures to confess:

Mark 11:22: **And Jesus replying said to them, Have faith in God (constantly).** (Have faith in God; trust Him.)

Mark 11:23: **Truly, I tell you, whoever says to this mountain, Be lifted up and thrown into the sea! and** does not doubt at all in his heart, but believes that what he says will take place, it will be done for him. (Say: "Mountain of scars of abuse, be removed!")

Mark 11:24: **For this reason I am telling you, whatever you ask for in prayer, believe — trust and be confident — that it is granted to you, and you will [get it].** (Get ready to receive!)

Mark 11:25: **And whenever you stand praying, if you have anything against any one, forgive him *and* let it drop — leave it, let it go — in order that your Father Who is in heaven may also forgive you your [own] failings *and* shortcomings *and* let them drop.** (Most importantly, when you want something from God, *you must first forgive* to be set free.)

One more word about freeing yourself. Many times people begin to feel sorry for themselves because they really do "put up with" a lot in their circumstances, therefore giving them a good excuse for self-pity — for having a "pity party." They are saying in essence, "Feel sorry for me; I have it so bad!" Well, maybe they do. Maybe you do too. Perhaps your circumstances are unbearable, maybe your situation does seem hopeless. But feeling sorry for yourself doesn't help anything! It makes nothing better — it changes nothing except to help you sink even deeper into hopelessness and helplessness. You must choose to be victorious in your attitude in spite of your circumstances.

According to *The American College Dictionary*, the word *circumstance* comes from a word referring to "surrounding condition." Just make the right choice and you are on your way to getting yourself free from whatever condition is encircling or surrounding you.

Scriptures to confess:

Proverbs 31:27: **She** (the righteous woman) **looks well to how things go in her household, and the bread of** idleness (gossip, discontent and self-pity) she will not eat.

STEP 5: CONFESS YOURSELF
(Make positive, optimistic, God-filled confessions about yourself)

Proverbs 31 is the outline of what God has made available to women, telling us what characteristics we are to have in our lives. In the back of this book I have included a guideline to help you make positive confessions based on this passage. I have also included an outline of scriptural confessions entitled "Delight Yourself." If you will read and confess these over and over, I believe you'll begin to see them become a reality in your life.

This step is where you need to take authority through confession over the curse of abuse that has dominated your life. Whether it was passed on to you from former generations or whether the devil found a loophole in your life to begin the curse with you, *you must* stop it.

Say: "In Jesus' name, I speak directly to the curse of abuse that has been in my life. You will not pass down from generation to generation. You will not continue into my children. I call you null and void this minute, this hour, this date, the _____ day of _____ (month) of the year 19__. You will not go any farther. You have no more power. You have no more place. In the name of Jesus Christ, my Lord and Savior, I declare it to be so. In Jesus' name and through His blood I pronounce that I am free from the curse — and so are all the generations to follow me."

STEP 6: PRAISE YOURSELF (Say: "I am somebody special to God")

John 3:16: **For God so greatly loved *and* dearly prized the world that He [even] gave up His only-begotten (unique) Son, so that whoever believes in (trusts, clings to, relies on) Him shall not perish — come to destruction, be lost — but have eternal (everlasting) life.**

Say: "God loves me and believes in me."

Proverbs 31:11: **The heart of her husband trusts in her confidently *and* relies on and believes in her safely, so that he has no lack of *honest* gain or need of *dishonest* spoil.**

Say: "I am a Proverbs 31 woman. Each day I am becoming more of what I was created to be. I am precious and valuable."

Psalm 139:14: **I will praise thee; for I am fearfully *and* wonderfully made: marvellous *are* thy works; and *that* my soul knoweth right well** (KJV).

Say: "I am 'wonderfully *and* fearfully' made."

Isaiah 54:17: ***But* no weapon that is formed against you shall prosper, and every tongue that shall rise against you in judgment you shall show to be in the wrong. This [peace, righteousness, security, triumph over opposition] is the heritage of the servants of the Lord [those in whom the ideal**

Servant of the Lord is reproduced]. This is the righteousness *or* the vindication which they obtain from Me — this is that which I impart to them as their justification — says the Lord.

Say: "I am born to win — to overcome! No weapon formed against me shall prosper."

Isaiah 54:13: **And all your [spiritual] children shall be disciples — taught of the Lord [and obedient to His will]; and great shall be the peace *and* undisturbed composure of your children.**

Say: "I shall be taught of the Lord, and great shall be my peace and undisturbed composure."

2 Timothy 1:7: **For God did not give us a spirit of timidity — of cowardice, of craven and cringing and fawning fear — but [He has given us a spirit] of power and of love and of calm *and* well-balanced mind *and* discipline *and* self-control.**

Say: "God has not given me the spirit of fear but of *power*, *love*, and *sound* mind."

2 Corinthians 5:21: **For our sake He made Christ [virtually] to be sin Who knew no sin, so that in *and* through Him we might become [endued with, viewed as in and examples of] the righteousness of God — what we ought to be, approved and acceptable and in right relationship with Him, by His goodness.**

Say: "I am the righteousness of God."

Matthew 6:33: **But seek (aim at and strive after) first of all His kingdom, and His righteousness [His way of doing and being right], and then all these things taken together will be given you besides.**

Say: "I now seek first the Kingdom of God and His righteousness, and all these things shall be added unto me."

Philippians 4:19: **And my God**

will liberally supply (fill to the full) your every need according to His riches in glory in Christ Jesus.**

Say: "My God shall supply *all* of my needs according to His riches in glory."

Philippians 4:11: **Not that I am implying that I was in any personal want, for I have learned how to be content (satisfied to the point where I am not disturbed or disquieted) in whatever state I am.**

Say: "I have learned that whatever state I am in therewith to be content."

STEP 7: LIFT YOURSELF (Be happy with yourself)

Say: "*I choose to be happy.* I choose to pray. I choose to be thankful. I choose to let the Holy Ghost have full reign in my life."

Scriptures to confess:

Psalm 37:4: **Delight yourself also in the Lord, and He will give you the** desires *and* secret petitions of your heart.

Isaiah 58:14: **Then shall you delight yourself in the Lord, and I will make you to ride on the high places of the earth, and I will feed you with the heritage [promised for you to] Jacob your father; for the mouth of the Lord has spoken it.**

Isaiah 60:1: **Arise [from the depression and prostration in which circumstances have kept you; rise to a new life]! Shine — be radiant with the glory of the Lord; for your light is come, and the glory of the Lord is risen upon you!**

Proverbs 15:3: **The eyes of the Lord are in every place, keeping watch upon the evil and the good.**

Proverbs 15:4: **A gentle tongue [with its healing power] is a tree of life, but willful contrariness in it breaks down the spirit.**

Proverbs 15:5: **A fool despises his father's instruction *and* correction, but** he who regards reproof acquires prudence.

Proverbs 15:30: **The light in the eyes [of him whose heart is joyful] rejoices the hearts of others, and good news nourishes the bones.**

Proverbs 16:24: **Pleasant words are as a honeycomb, sweet to the mind and healing to the body.**

Proverbs 17:22: **A happy heart is good medicine *and* a cheerful mind works healing, but a broken spirit dries the bones.**

1 Thessalonians 5:16-19: **Be happy [in your faith] *and* rejoice *and* be gladhearted continually — always.**

Be unceasing in prayer — praying perseveringly;

Thank [God] in everything — no matter what the circumstances may be, be thankful and give thanks; for this is the will of God for you [who are] in Christ Jesus [the Revealer and Mediator of that will].

ABUSE: Bruised but Not Broken!

Do not quench (suppress or subdue) the (Holy) Spirit.

STEP 8: HELP YOURSELF (Be truthful with yourself)

One way you can help yourself is to listen to yourself. Make sure you are speaking positive words over yourself. Stand in front of the mirror and say good things about yourself.

Write down ten positive things about yourself and say them out loud.

Ten Positive Confessions:

1.
2.
3.
4.
5.
6.
7.
8.
9.

10.

STEP 9: TRUST YOURSELF
(Know you are trustworthy)

Proverbs 31:11 says that *you are trustworthy,* so trust yourself to make the right decisions. Learn to pray and listen to the voice of the Holy Ghost and His leadings. Listen to the voice of the Father. Listen to Jesus. All three Persons of the Trinity will lead you and guide you if you will just learn (by practicing) to listen to them. They give good and accurate advice.

STEP 10: LOVE YOURSELF
(Know that you are so valuable that no price can be placed on you)

...you shall love your neighbor as yourself...(Lev. 19:18). God would never tell you to hate your neighbor, would He? That's why He said to love your neighbor "as yourself," because He wants you to love yourself — to know what a prize you are — to know how valuable you are. A possession is prized and valued according to the price that was paid for it. The life of the only Son of God, Jesus, was paid for you. That makes you priceless — invaluable! *You are so valuable that no price can be placed on you!* You are worth more than you think! You are worth loving! You are priceless to God. And you need to love yourself in order to fulfill God's Word!

You must learn to love yourself before anyone else can learn to love you. You bind up everyone else's love by not freeing your own love to yourself.

Spend time with yourself.

Scriptures to confess:

Leviticus 19:18: **You shall not take revenge or bear any grudge against the sons of your people, but you shall love your neighbor as yourself. I am the Lord.**

Well, now that you've been through each step, how do you feel? I pray you can feel the very presence of God inside you and that your shoulders are squared back and you are standing taller on the outside and on the inside.

Remember to *make the choice* to practice these ten steps. Choices affect your health and your emotions. Your entire life is dictated by the choices you make.

Now I want to leave you with this very sobering thought. The devil will tell you, "You don't need to know this stuff," because it is his desire to "cloak you with stupidity." Even though you would never choose to be stupid, the devil will try to put this cloak upon you. You have to *choose* to throw it off and get knowledge. God says, **My people are destroyed for lack of knowledge...**(Hos. 4:6.)

God has given us a contract with Him — the Bible. The devil cannot break the contract because it is legal through Jesus. The contract says: "This is your day. You can rise up. You are somebody to God, and He can do and wants to do great and wonderful things in you and through you as you take authority in the name of Jesus and say, 'This is my contract, and the devil can't break it. In the name of Jesus, I am somebody!'"

I want to end this book with a prayer for you for your continued healing:

"Father, thank You for loving each of us. Thank You, Lord, that You are a good God. Help us, Lord, to keep our eyes centered in on You at all times.

"Father, help us to remember as we focus in on You that You will help us to deal with the situations and circumstances of our lives in the present *and the past*. Thank You, Lord, for stretching out Your finger of healing, right now, and running over the scars in our emotions, our minds, our memories and our bodies.

"Thank You, Lord, for pulling off the 'scabs' in our lives, even though the exposed wound is very painful. Thank You, Lord, for going right into the wound and healing it from the very tip of the root all the way to the surface, leaving nothing for the devil to throw in our faces later on!

"I love You, Lord, and I trust You to take care of us as we choose to be set completely free! Yes, we do choose now to be continually healed of all the hurt within us, in the precious name of Jesus.

"Thank You, Lord. I love You. Amen."

ABUSE: Bruised but Not Broken!

The Proverbs 31 Woman

Proverbs 31:10-31:

V. 10: I am capable.
 I am intelligent.
 I am virtuous.
 I am more precious than jewels.
 I am more valuable than rubies or pearls.

v. 11: I am trustworthy.
 I am reliable.

v. 12: I am good.

vv. 13,14: I am hardworking.

v. 15: I am disciplined.
 I am spiritual.

v. 16: I make time to pray and grow.
 I am an organizer.
 I am smart in business.
 I am a seed-planter in every part of my life.

vv. 17-19: I am in good physical shape.

v. 20: I am giving.
    I am compassionate.
    I never doubt, but I have great faith.

vv. 21,22: My family and I wear the best.

v. 23: I am an asset to my husband.

v. 24: I not only dress well, but I am a good designer and
    I sell these clothes.

v. 25: I am strong.
    I am dignified and secure.
    I look to the future.
    I am prepared.

v. 26: I speak wisely.
    I have a kind tongue when giving counsel and instruction.

v. 27: I watch over my household.
    I am not idle.
    I do not gossip.
    I am content.
    I do not live in self-pity.

vv. 28-31: My children call me blessed.
   My husband boasts of me and
      praises me.
   I am a woman who reverently and
      worshipfully fears the Lord.

Delight Yourself

Psalm 37:4: God is an "if-then" God. He says: "If you will do this, then I will do that. If you will *delight yourself* in Me, then I will give you the *desires of your heart.*"

Isaiah 58:14: *Delight Yourself.* If you will delight yourself in the Lord, then He will make you to ride on the high places of the earth, and He will feed you with the heritage promised for you to Jacob your father.

1 Thessalonians 5:16-19,23,24:

v. 16: Choose to be happy. (Emotional realm)

v. 17: Choose to pray. (Spiritual and physical realm)

v. 18: Choose to be thankful. (Mental realm)

v. 19: Choose not to quench the Holy Ghost. (Supernatural realm)

v. 23: If you choose to do these things, then God will sanctify you, separate you, make you pure and wholly consecrated to Him. He will preserve your (human) spirit, soul and body.

v. 24. Choose to trust God.

Good positive scriptures of choices:

Proverbs 15:4: **A gentle tongue [with its healing power] is a tree of life, but willful contrariness in it breaks down the spirit.**

Proverbs 15:13: **A glad heart makes a cheerful countenance, but by sorrow of heart the spirit is broken.**

Proverbs 15:15: **All the days of the desponding afflicted are made evil [by anxious thoughts and foreboding], but he who has a glad heart has a continual feast [regardless of circumstances].**

Isaiah 60:1: **Arise [from the depression and prostration in which circumstances have kept you; rise to a new life]! Shine — be radiant with the glory of the Lord; for your light is come, and the glory of the Lord is risen upon you!**

Proverbs 15:30: **The light in the eyes [of him whose heart is joyful] rejoices the heart of others,** *and* **good news nourishes the bones.**

Proverbs 16:24: **Pleasant words are as a honeycomb, sweet to the mind and healing to the body.**

Proverbs 17:22: **A happy heart is a good medicine** *and* **a cheerful mind works healing, but a broken spirit dries the bones.**

Choices affect your health.

Choices affect your emotions.

**Chery's books are available
from your local bookstore
or from:**

Praise
BOOKS
P.O. Box 35035
Tulsa, OK 74153

Order Form

If you would like more teaching on making the right choices to become all you can be and take charge of your life — or if you have a friend or loved one who needs help in a certain area of his or her life, just write for some of these materials.

Cheryl Prewitt-Salem

"Take Charge of Your Life" Library

Books   **Quantity**

You Are Somebody..............................$5.95 ____
(This is great for abuse victims or those who have developed a poor self-image for many different reasons.)

A Bright and Shining Place ....$6.95 ____
(This is my life story of how God raised me from a crippled little girl in Choctaw County, Mississippi, to Miss America 1980.

It will show you what making the right choices can do for you!)

ABUSE:
Bruised but Not Broken! ....$2.95 ____
(You may desire more copies of this book to have at work or home, or to carry with you so you can practice the Ten Steps and the "Proverbs 31 Woman" and "Delight Yourself" confessions — or you may want some copies for friends or loved ones.)

Mini-books

Health and Beauty Secrets...................$.75 ____
(This little book is very practical in answering questions concerning health and beauty. These tips I share can help you become the best YOU that you can be!)

Choose to be Happy ....$.75 ____
(This book is small, but powerful. It holds the secret to being happy *all the time*. It's great for people in all walks of life.)

Simple Facts: Salvation, Healing and the Holy Ghost..$.75 ____
(This book gives you the steps to take once you've been saved, baptized with the Holy Spirit [speaking in tongues], or healed, to make sure you develop the way God wants you to.)

Tapes

*You Can Be the Best You
That You Can Be!* ....$19.95____
(Four-part teaching series on self-image.
Two tapes on self-image, one tape on health
and beauty secrets, plus a music tape
entitled *Living Proof*.)

Choose to be Happy ....$8.00____
(All-music cassette with happy songs.)

*Ain't Nothin' Gonna
Stop You Now* ....$8.00____
(All-motivational music cassette.)

*The Music &
Ministry of Cheryl* ....$8.00____
(Live testimony of healing, winning Miss
America, and four songs on cassette.)

Living Proof ....$8.00____
(All-music cassette from "Richard Roberts
Live" telecast, including "Devil, Pick on
Somebody Your Own Size," "I'm Not
Lettin' Myself Get Down," and many
more.)

Videos

"Take Charge of Your Life with Cheryl and
Friends" ....$19.95____
(High-impact aerobics video.)

"Get Ready with Cheryl
and Friends" ....$19.95 ____
(Low-impact aerobics video.)

Total Amount Enclosed:........................$____

Just clip this order form and mail with your check or money order to:

**Cheryl Prewitt-Salem
P.O. Box 701287
Tulsa, OK 74170
(918) 495-6424**

If you have any questions or comments, just write or call. Please feel free to include your prayer requests.

Please print:

Name _____

Address _____

City _____

State_____**Zip** _____